THE GOLDEN YEARS

1966

text: David Sandison, Michael Heatley, Lorna Milne, Ian Welch

design: Paul Kurzeja

SIENA

Welcome to The Golden Years and the vast mosaic of events which made up 1966. It was a fascinating puzzle at the time, but we can now look back at it all to get a clear picture of what really was going on, and how it would help shape our future.

It wasn't a good year for any world leader who fancied a quiet time, that's for sure. Having decided to commit US forces into the Vietnam conflict, President Johnson now had to deal with the awful reality of his decision as the Vietcong proved themselves more than a match for the might of the US military machine. Nearer home, he had to deal with the racial violence which erupted in America's cities.

In Britain, a re-elected Harold Wilson learned that Prime Ministers had to be able to juggle too. A rash of strikes, continued tension in Ulster and the vexatious problems which the Rhodesian rebels caused, all conspired to give him long workdays and precious little time to relax.

India, the world's largest democracy, found itself a new and dynamic leader when Mrs Indira Gandhi succeeded Lal Shastri as only the second woman in history to be elected to such a position of power. The people of the Soviet Union, the world's second-largest

non-democracy, woke up to find that the very unelected Leonid Brezhnev was now their supremo. And the people of China, the world's largest non-democracy, awoke one day to learn that Mao Tse-tung had let loose the Red Guards to pitch the nation into an unimagined hell of suspicion, arrest, disruption and anarchic chaos.

Delight swept through England in July as the national soccer team carried off the World Cup in a six-goal thriller against West Germany. It was also the year when it was officially confirmed that the sixties were swingin', and that London was the swingingest city of them all! Good reading!

Beatle George Marries Model Patti Boyd

THERE WERE BROKEN female teenaged hearts all over the world today when The Beatles' lead guitarist, George Harrison, married actress and fashion model Patti Boyd at a quiet ceremony near his Epsom, Surrey, home.

To avoid screaming fans, the wedding was kept so secret that fellow group members John Lennon and Ringo Starr were on holiday and therefore unable to attend. Paul McCartney - now the only bachelor Beatle, though he and actress Jane Asher were generally accepted as an item - was able to attend, however.

The couple had met nearly two years earlier on the set of the Fab Four's film *A Hard Day's Night,* in which Patti appeared as a schoolgirl. The Harrisons' marriage was not to last, however. After inspiring George's best friend, blues guitarist Eric Clapton, to write his best-known song, *Layla,* about her, Patti would marry him in 1979.

Britain To Have Breath Test

New Year, New Ruler: Bokassa Takes Power

Jean Bedel Bokassa became the new ruler of the Central African Republic on the first day of the new year, following the coup in which his cousin, former leader David Dacko, was overthrown.

The 45 year old Colonel soon began to increase his hold on the country and, during his subsequent thirteen years in power, would emerge as a harsh dictator. His most heinous crime would be the massacre, in 1979, of a hundred schoolchildren who'd been demonstrating against having to wear school uniform.

With the number of accidents caused by drunken drivers on the increase, the British Government today published a bill to introduce the random testing of motorists. The 'breathalyser' test, which could be carried out on the spot, would make it possible to measure the quantity of alcohol present in the motorist's blood. If that proved to be higher than 80 milligrams per 100cc of blood, the driver would be liable to prosecution. Motoring organizations were quick to claim that the proposed law constituted an infringement of civil liberties, but Britain's pedestrians – so often the innocent victims of drunken driving – seemed unlikely to agree.

Massive Sea Hunt As US Loses H-Bomb

The terrible prospect of an accidental nuclear explosion gripped the world today when a US Air Force B-52 bomber carrying an H-bomb collided in mid-air over Spain with a K-C 135 fuel tanker aircraft, and crashed into the Atlantic off the southern Spanish coast.

Eight of the B-52's 14-man crew were killed in the crash, which left US military chiefs with the task of mounting an immediate hunt to locate the wreckage and the H-bomb. Leading the search were Strategic Air Command aircraft.

It would not be until April that a midget submarine located and recovered the bomb intact, but US officials had to calm local fears of radiation leakage by swimming in the sea at the crash site!

ARRIVALS
Born this month:
21: Wendy James,
UK rock singer, songwriter

DEPARTURES
Died this month:
1: Vincent Auriol, French statesman, President 1945-53, aged 82
11: Lal Bahadur Shastri, Indian statesman, Prime Minister 1964-66, aged 63; Alberto Giacometti, Swiss sculptor, aged 64
14: Sergei Korolev, Soviet engineer, aged 59
16: Alhaji Sir Abubakar Tafawa Balewa, Nigerian chief, politician, Prime Minister 1960-66, aged 53

JANUARY 19

Aussie PM Menzies Ends Record Reign

Sir Robert Menzies, the Australian Prime Minister, resigned in Canberra today, after 16 years in office – the longest on record. A barrister by profession, Menzies was first elected to the Federal House of Representatives in 1934 and – in something of a meteoric rise – became Attorney-General the following year, a post which he held for four years.

He was first elected Prime Minister in 1939, although on that occasion he remained in the post for just two years. In 1949 he was elected premier of the new coalition government which had swept the Labour Party from power. Sir Robert's time in office, during which he established strong links with Western nations and directed the increasingly thriving Australian economy, was marked by his personal qualities of integrity and warmth.

JANUARY 31

Rhodesia Crisis Deepens – Smith Expels British MPs

THE BOMBSHELL CAUSED by Ian Smith's Rhodesian Front government's unilateral declaration of independence from Britain last November continued to cause ever-widening ripples. The move – a result of the rebel government's refusal to introduce majority rule – had been condemned by the United Nations and resulted in the Board of Trade in London placing a ban on trade between the two countries today.

Earlier in the month, the Commonwealth Conference in Lagos had degenerated into a slanging match when the Prime Minister of Sierra Leone demanded that Britain take military action. British PM Harold Wilson vehemently opposed the suggestion, saying that sending in troops was logistically difficult and likely to cause widespread bloodshed.

If the experiences of the three Labour MPs who visited the country on a 'fact-finding mission' were any indication, he was probably right. Although they succeeded in securing an audience with Ian Smith, on January 12 their hotel was invaded by a large crowd of white protesters, and they were jostled and abused. Rescued by plain-clothes policemen, the MPs were expelled from Rhodesia the following day.

JANUARY 3

Eric's The Mann For Manfred... Temporarily!

Rumours abounded of a new rock supergroup tonight when Eric Burdon of The Animals appeared as lead singer of Manfred Mann at London's legendary Marquee Club. In fact, Manfred Mann's regular lead singer, Paul Jones, was recovering from a recent car accident, and the Newcastle wild man's recruitment was but temporary. Later in the year, however, rumour would become fact when Jones left the Manfreds, seduced by the twin prizes of a solo career and film fame - he was to star, with supermodel Jean Shrimpton, in *Privilege*. His replacement, on a permanent basis, was Mike d'Abo, formerly of The Band Of Angels.

Indira Is India's Choice

Following the sudden death, in Tashkent on January 11, of Indian Prime Minister Lal Shastri from a heart attack, Mrs Indira Gandhi (Pictured being sworn in by President Radhakrishnan) was elected to succeed him today. Mrs Gandhi's pedigree for the post was more than adequate, being the daughter of Jawaharlal Nehru, India's first Prime Minister. Indeed the Nehru 'dynasty' had hardly been broken by the brief two-year period of Shastri's premiership. Mrs Gandhi, aged 48, was a popular choice, beating her only opponent Morarji Desai by 355 votes to 199. She had already promised to continue the work of her father, saying she would strive to create what he used to call 'a climate of peace'.

Her first proof of sincerity came when she confirmed that she would honour the peace agreement with Pakistan that Mr Shastri had negotiated in Tashkent only hours before he died.

Chaplin's Rival, Buster Keaton, Dies

THE WORLD OF FILM comedy lost a giant of the craft today when Buster Keaton (pictured), the American movie comedian, succumbed to lung cancer in Los Angeles at the age of 70. Like Charlie Chaplin, his greatest rival, Keaton was the champion of the little man, constantly pitting his wits against his superiors and an increasingly impersonal, machine-dominated world.

Renowned for his acrobatic performances, Joseph Francis Keaton began his showbiz career performing in his family's travelling medicine show, where his tough fall-about style earned him his nickname. In 1917, he made his first movie with 'Fatty' Arbuckle, and spent the 1920s devising and performing in a string of classic silent comedies, among them *The Navigator*, *The Playhouse* and *The General*.

However, the 1920s proved to be his heyday, and personal problems - exacerbated by alcoholism - dogged him during the next two decades. In the 1950s, the occasional cameo role, coupled with the re-release of his earlier films, revived his reputation as one of America's foremost comics and an innovative genius.

Nuclear TV Drama Causes Shock Waves

The controversial television film, *The War Game*, which showed the horrific effects of a nuclear attack on British cities, was finally screened at the National Film Theatre in London tonight.

Originally banned by the BBC programme chiefs - who had commissioned the drama - following governmental pressure, the screening attracted demonstrations by CND supporters who objected to the BBC's ban.

Both sides, however, agreed that *The War Game*, for which director Peter Watkins used genuine German footage of the firestorm which destroyed Dresden at the end of World War II, and amateur actors for veracity, aroused strong emotions in a decade when the threat of atomic obliteration was deeply rooted in the national psyche.

Music World Misses Red-Hot Sophie

Sophie Tucker – who, for years, had been singing *One of These Days (You're Gonna Miss Me, Honey)* – died today at the age of 79.

The singer with the earthy style once called 'The Last of the Red Hot Mamas', was born to a Russian-Jewish farming family which later emigrated to the US, where she took to the boards on the vaudeville theatre and cabaret circuits. An immediate hit, she would become one of the world's most popular and highly-paid entertainers in a career which would last nearly 60 years.

UK TOP 10 SINGLES

1: You Were On My Mind
- Crispian St Peters
2: Spanish Flea
- Herb Alpert
3: These Boots Are Made For Walkin'
- Nancy Sinatra
4: Love's Just A Broken Heart
- Cilla Black
5: A Groovy Kind Of Love
- The Mindbenders
6: Michelle
- The Overlanders
7: Keep On Runnin'
- The Spencer Davis Group
8: 19th Nervous Breakdown
- The Rolling Stones
9: A Must To Avoid
- Herman's Hermits
10: Mirror Mirror
- Pinkerton's Assorted Colours

FEBRUARY 24

Nkrumah Ousted While Seeking Peace

President Kwame Nkrumah (pictured) of Ghana arrived in the Chinese capital, Beijing, today, was welcomed by a host of dignitaries and a 21-gun salute...and the news that he had been toppled by an army coup in Accra.

Nkrumah, who was *en route* to Vietnam, where he'd intended to try to broker a peace deal between the US and North Vietnam, announced his intention of carrying on to Hanoi.

He had been Ghana's president since the country became independent in 1957, but had established a reputation as a hard man. Sentenced to death in his absence, he would not return to Ghana.

Lift-Off Time For Freddie's Cut-Price Airline

BRITISH TOURISTS GAINED a new hero today when Freddie Laker, the ebullient entrepreneur, announced that he was setting up a new airline designed to cash in on the burgeoning package holiday market.

He had already proved his ability during five years as manager of British United Airways, which had become Britain's largest independent airline in that time, and had purchased three BAC One-Eleven jets at a cost of more than £1 million each.

Laker, a self-made millionaire who'd started out with a mere £40 ($60) pay-off from the Royal Air Force, was promising the travelling public longer and cheaper holidays.

He succeeded in his aim and would later pioneer cheap flights across the Atlantic with his Skytrain service. Sadly, he would be forced out of the air travel business in the 1980s – unfairly squeezed out, he claimed, by a price-fixing deal between his larger competitors.

Peggy Fleming Wins Gold

American figure skater Peggy Gale Fleming clinched the gold medal at the World Figure Skating Championships in Switzerland this evening to take the world title for the first time in her career.

Fleming, who was born in 1948, won her first US Ladies' Championship at the tender age of 15, the first of five such wins, and her graceful style was to earn her gold in the 1968 Olympics. Having risen to the very peak of her sport, she subsequently turned to professional performance.

England Tame Germany In World Cup Warm-Up

England's football team continued their build-up to this summer's World Cup finals by defeating West Germany 1-0 in front of 75,000 fans at Wembley Stadium. The match was notable for the début of Geoff Hurst, West Ham United's 24 year old striker, who was regarded as a possible replacement for the out-of-sorts Jimmy Greaves.

England, who experimented tonight with a new 4-3-3 formation which purists weren't sure had much of a future, had already beaten Spain 2-0 in Madrid last December.

Apollo Space Programme Blasts Off

The launch of NASA's first Apollo test rocket from Cape Kennedy today proved a resounding success, though celebrations were cut short two days later when the last days of the Gemini Project were marred by the deaths of astronauts Elliott See Jr and Charles Bassett during training.

The Gemini Project, which had run from 1964 as a preparation for the Apollo moon programme, was designed to test man's ability to survive in space and to improve the manoeuvrability of spacecraft. In 1965-6 a total of ten manned flights were made, leading to the first ever space walk, in June 1965.

MAR

Arkle Wins Third Gold Cup In A Row

ARKLE, RATED BY MANY as the greatest steeplechaser of all time, entered the world record books with a vengeance today when he won the Cheltenham Gold Cup - the greatest prize in the British National Hunt horse-racing calendar - for the third year running.

Bred and trained in Ireland, and owned by Anne, Duchess of Westminster, Arkle enjoyed a relatively easy win today, and certainly easier than his victories in previous years over his arch-rival, Mill House.

With Mill House out of the running this year, the champion – ridden by jockey Pat Taaffe – romped to victory, passing the winning post a clear 30 lengths ahead of the rest of the field, and notching up his 25th steeplechase win in the process.

Pickles Ends Lost World Cup Pickle

A tiny mongrel called Pickles (pictured) saved a lot of red faces in the English Football Association today when he found the Jules Rimet Trophy - the World Cup - in a South London garden, seven days after it was stolen from a display case in Westminster Central Hall.

Pickles, who was out for his daily constitutional with his owner, a Thames lighterman called David Corbett, unearthed the solid gold trophy when he began tearing at the newspaper it had been wrapped in by whoever stole it.

With 16 nations due to play for the World Cup in England four months later, the loss of the actual object the victorious captain would wave aloft on July 30 was a severe embarrassment to English football bigwigs.

Loudmouth Lennon In 'Blasphemy' Bombshell

Outspoken Beatle John Lennon put his foot in it today when, in an interview with pop journalist Maureen Cleave for the *London Evening Standard*, he expressed the opinion that his group was 'more popular than Jesus right now'.

The remark passed without much comment in Britain, but was made much of by the US media and resulted in public record-burning, demonstrations and even Ku Klux Klan threats, when a teen magazine reprinted it.

An obviously chastened Lennon would be forced to make a full and contrite apology at the press conference that started their US tour in August, the last the band would ever undertake.

US Astronauts In Space Docking Drama

US astronauts Neil Armstrong and David Scott made their own piece of history today when they became the first men to dock their spacecraft with another while in orbit. Triumph turned to drama, however, when a rocket on their Gemini 8 craft fired prematurely and put it in a wild spin.

The rendezvous in space - between the Gemini 8 and the final stage of the Agena launcher which had put them into orbit - was a key preparation for the US plan to put a man on the moon before 1970.

When the Gemini rocket fired, Armstrong was forced to undock the craft earlier than planned, and returned to a Pacific splash-down two days before schedule.

UK TOP 10 SINGLES

1: A Groovy Kind Of Love
- The Mindbenders
2: Sha La La La Lee
- The Small Faces
3: Barbara Ann
- The Beach Boys
4: These Boots Are Made For Walkin'
- Nancy Sinatra
5: Backstage
- Gene Pitney
6: I Can't Let Go
- The Hollies
7: The Sun Ain't Gonna Shine Anymore
- The Walker Brothers
8: 19th Nervous Breakdown
- The Rolling Stones
9: My Love
- Petula Clark
10: Spanish Flea
- Herb Alpert

Born this month:
19: Andy Sinton, UK football player; Nigel Clough, England international football player
23: Marti Pellow (Mark McLoughlin), UK pop star (Wet Wet Wet)
25: Anton Rogan, Northern Ireland international football player

DEPARTURES

Died this month:
30: Maxfield Parrish, US artist, aged 95; Erwin Piscator, German theatre director, aged 72

MARCH 29

Brezhnev, New Soviet Supremo, Slams US

In Moscow today, Leonid Brezhnev - the newly appointed First Secretary of the Soviet Communist Party, and so undisputed supremo of the regime - set the tone for his leadership with a thorough denouncement of the US military involvement in south-east Asia. In his opening speech to the 23rd Party Congress, he condemned what he called America's 'policy of aggression' in Vietnam.

Brezhnev had served his political apprenticeship under the dictator Josef Stalin and his reforming successor, Nikita Khrushchev, holding a variety of posts within the party in the Ukraine, Moldavia, and Kazakhstan.

After Khrushchev was ousted for his radical policy reforms and attacks on party bureaucracy in October 1964, Brezhnev became the prime mover in the resulting coalition.

MARCH 31

Anti-War Protests Escalate In US

Today's anti-war march down New York's Fifth Avenue was the biggest demonstration ever staged against the conflict in Vietnam, with more than 20,000 participating. The march – which attracted counter-demonstrations by egg-throwing protesters – was just one of many staged nationwide.

In Boston, yet more draft cards (military call-up papers) were burned by four protesters, exciting the anger of high school pupils who shouted 'Kill them! Shoot them!' in an unusual show of youthful support for their government's continued pursuit of the war.

MARCH 5

Green Berets Storm Pop Charts

Protest pop songs against the Vietnam War were nothing new – but the arrival of Sergeant Barry Sadler's *The Ballad Of The Green Berets* at the top of the US charts today added a new dimension to the argument. Inspired by Robin Moore's book *The Green Berets*, the patriotic ditty found Sadler reciting an ode to 'fighting men…America's best', and the US public responded by keeping the record in the charts for a full 13 weeks. A similarly gung-ho *Green Berets* LP would top the US album charts the following week. Sadler would hit the headlines again with his involvement in shooting incidents in 1978 and 1981.

Anglicans And Catholics Reconciled After 400 Years

THE SPLENDOUR OF Michelangelo's Sistine Chapel was the magnificent setting for today's historic reconciliation of a 400-year schism between the Anglican Church in the United Kingdom and the Roman Church. Although representatives of the two sides had met unofficially in 1960, the reception by Pope Paul of the Archbishop of Canterbury, Michael Ramsey, (pictured) represented the first official indication of an attempt at Christian unity.

One topic said to have been the subject of heated discussion was that of mixed marriages between Catholics and Protestants. However, the Vatican's previously hard line was softened just five days earlier when the Pope announced the ending of ex-communication as a penalty for such unions.

The Pope described the Churches' new relationship as a 'bridge of respect, of esteem and of charity'. Unfortunately, charity was low on the agenda of the three Anglican ministers who today described the Archbishop as 'a traitor to Protestant Britain' when they interrupted him celebrating Communion.

BATTLE ROYAL AS STAGE DRAMAS FIGHT IT OUT FOR SCREEN HONOURS

Critics of the Academy Awards (always thick on the ground) were particularly incensed this year when the two big films battling it out for Oscars turned out to be adaptations of works originally written for, and successes on, the stage. Where, they asked, were the original stories written only with wide-screen projection in mind? The answer, as ever, lay in the rejection trays of many a big studio mogul.

So it was that the main contenders in the 1966 Hollywood beanfeast were the equally-powerful *A Man For All Seasons* and *Who's Afraid Of Virginia Woolf*?

Alright, so the Best Picture list also included *Alfie, The Sand Pebbles* and *The Russians Are Coming, The Russians Are Coming*, but they were always bound to be also-rans - especially the latter, arguably the least funny comedy ever made.

Compared to the class acts of Robert Bolt's *A Man For All Seasons* and Edward Albee's *Virginia Woolf*, most of this year's offerings were ho-hum cannon fodder, although the inclusion of Antonioni's *Blow-Up* and Claude Lelouche's *A Man And A Woman* proved that some of the Academy members retained a degree of discernment.

In the end, while *A Man For All* Seasons emerged triumphant with the Best Picture prize, an Oscar for director Fred Zinneman, a well-deserved Best Actor statuette for Paul Scofield, an Adapted Screenplay trophy for Robert Bolt, one for photographer Ted Moore and another for costume designers Elizabeth Jaffenden and Joan Bridge, *Who's Afraid Of Virginia Woolf*? scored enough wins to make the honours pretty well even.

Elizabeth Taylor put on 20 lbs in weight and added a previously unseen venom to emerge as Best Actress, while Sandy Dennis twitched and stammered her way to a well-deserved Supporting Actress Oscar. Richard Burton, of course, lost out to Paul Scofield and so stopped *Virginia Woolf* enjoying a clean sweep of acting honours.

Actually, that's not strictly true. George Segal was nominated, as Supporting Actor for his portrayal of Sandy Dennis' husband, but he mysteriously lost out to Walter Matthau, who won for the forgettable and otherwise un-nominated *The Fortune Cookie*.

Equally mysteriously, while her older sister, Vanessa, was producing excellent performances in *Blow-Up* and *Morgan!*, Lynn Redgrave was collecting a Best Actress nomination for the fairly dire Swinging London tragi-comedy *Georgy Girl*.

Claude Lelouche did collect an Oscar for *A Man And*

A Woman, which won the Best Foreign Film award, and also shared the Original Screenplay prize with Pierre Uytterhoeven.

The film song of the year turned out to be *Born Free*, the Don Black/John Barry composition. Added to the Oscar he was awarded for his score for the same film, the British-born John Barry had every reason not to return any calls he might have had from his bank manager for a day or two.

Footnote: winner of this year's Feature Documentary Oscar was *The War Game*, Peter Watkin's stunning and disturbing vision of how Britain would fare in the case of World War III. Made for the BBC, it remained unscreened on British television. Too scary, said 'The Men In Charge'. Too accurate, said the Campaign for Nuclear Disarmament.

APRIL

APRIL 1

Labour Is Re-Elected

The Labour Party was returned to power in Britain today with a majority of 96, ending two years of a small majority which had made it impossible to make the sweeping changes it wanted.

Prime Minister Harold Wilson claimed Labour now had a 'clear mandate' – although this was not necessarily good news for voters, with the prospect of unpalatable measures to restore Britain's economy to health.

Wilson, who spent his first years as premier increasing his profile as an international politician, was currently facing the crisis caused by Ian Smith's unilateral declaration of independence in Rhodesia. The election result was bad news for the Tory Party's new leader, Edward Heath. Having just succeeded Sir Alec Douglas-Home, he now faced the prospect of a long period in opposition.

APRIL 9

Sophia Loren Marries Carlo Ponti

Film actress Sophia Loren married her mentor, Italian film producer Carlo Ponti (pictured), today – for the second time! Their first wedding had taken place nearly ten years earlier in Mexico, exciting scandal in Italy where it was claimed that Ponti was still married to his first wife as Italy did not recognize divorce. With this earlier marriage annulled, the pair moved to France to begin the process of becoming naturalized French citizens, enabling Ponti to obtain a divorce. Despite the fact that Italian law had still not been changed, the small, private ceremony went ahead in Paris.

Mao Unleashes Cultural Revolution

THE CHINESE LEADER Mao Tse-tung announced a new campaign this month, designed to recreate the revolutionary enthusiasm of his victory over Chinese Nationalists in 1949 for a generation of Chinese too young to remember the early days of the country's transformation into the world's biggest communist state.

What was being called the Great Proletarian Cultural Revolution would, in reality, prove to be a concerted attempt by Mao to regain control of the bureaucracy in Chinese cultural life, and emerge victorious in a power struggle with head of state Liu Shao-chi.

The Cultural Revolution quickly became a disaster as Red Guards – young members of the Communist Party Mao had empowered to 'supervise' the upheaval – destroyed priceless works of art and valuable historical objects. Any sign of 'elitism' was stamped out by them. Schools and universities were shut, as teachers and other intellectuals were imprisoned or sent to work on the land in remote regions. All in all, the Cultural Revolution would prove a tragedy.

APRIL 10

Novelist Evelyn Signs Off

The world of letters lost one of its most distinctive members today when Evelyn Waugh, the satirist and novelist, died unexpectedly at his home in Combe Florey, Somerset at the age of 62. After gaining his first literary successes in the 1920s, he prospered greatly in the 1930s with *Vile Bodies* and *Black Mischief* before going on to write the nostalgic *Brideshead Revisited* and the black comedy *The Loved One*, among many others.

A journalist and a travel writer, Waugh nevertheless rejected those great definers of twentieth-century culture – radio and television. Married briefly, and bizarrely, to a woman with the same forename (Evelyn Gardner), he eventually married her cousin who bore him six children.

Although he was fond of criticizing the aristocracy, his later years were characterized by an increasing adoption of the more idiosyncratic and eccentric habits of that class, including boorish bad behaviour and virulent anti-Semitism.

Dr Zhivago Opens To Acclaim In London

DAVID LEAN'S STUNNING film *Dr Zhivago* received its première in London this month. Starring the British actress Julie Christie as the heroine, Lara, and Omar Sharif in the title role, this adaptation of Boris Pasternak's novel told an epic love story of a Moscow doctor, exiled and separated from the women he loved, as the Russian Revolution took it's course.

With beautiful and dramatic location photography and a haunting theme tune which immediately caught the imagination of the cinema-going public, *Dr Zhivago* would become the UK's top box-office attraction and be beaten only by the current James Bond thriller, *Thunderball*, in the United States.

As one critic put it: '*Dr Zhivago* does for snow what Lawrence Of Arabia did for sand.' And the film industry must have agreed, because it would scoop up no fewer than six Academy Award nominations.

APRIL 15

Official: London Is The Swingin' Capital

The world learned today what its citizens had known for some time already - London was swinging, and the younger generation had transformed its streets into a riot of colour, style and very exciting music.

Confirmation came in the current edition of the influential US news magazine *Time*, which, alerted that British rock stars were dominating the US charts and British fashion was transforming the way US teenagers looked and sounded, decided to take a good look at the city from which all this buzz was emanating. As the front cover article succinctly put it: 'In this century, every decade has its city…and for the Sixties that city is London.'

APRIL 17

Acid Guru Leary Arrested

Former Harvard psychology professor Timothy Leary (pictured), the most famous proponent of psychedelic drugs, was arrested and charged with the possession of narcotics when police raided his home in Dutchess County, New York, today. Leary had already been fired from his post at the prestigious Ivy League university because of his continued experiments with the hallucinogenic drug LSD, which he recommended for its consciousness-altering capabilities. In 1965, Leary had converted to Hinduism and in 1966 founded the League for Spiritual Discovery, coining the catch-phrase of the 1960s: 'Turn on, tune in, and drop out'. Today's arrest would not be Leary's last brush with the law and he would suffer exile abroad before serving a three-year prison sentence.

APRIL 19

Aussies Arrive To Aid US In Vietnam

The first military conscripts to leave Australia on active service since the end of the Korean War departed from Sydney today, the advance party for what would be an eventual 4,500-strong task force to reinforce the US war machine.

Qantas, the Australian state airline, was recruited to help with moving Australian troops to the South Vietnamese capital, Saigon. Sixteen scheduled flights to London were cancelled as the company became a ferry service for what an Australian Army spokesman described as 'a highly professional and specialized group'.

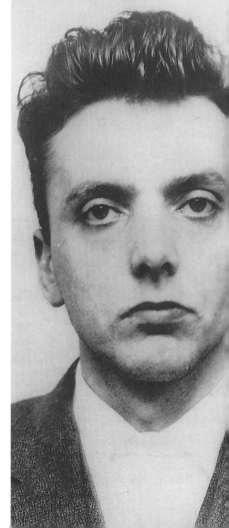

Life For Moors Murderers Brady And Hindley

IAN BRADY AND MYRA HINDLEY, the infamous couple known simply as the Moors Murderers, were sentenced to separate terms of life imprisonment in London's Old Bailey court today, despite the fact that the bodies of all their child victims had yet to be found.

Brady (pictured), the 28 year old acknowledged instigator of a sadistic regime of terror which resulted in the deaths of at least three, but probably more, children, received three concurrent life sentences, while Hindley - said to be Brady's 'willing accomplice' - was given two concurrent life sentences.

Police were first alerted to the duo's murderous activities by Myra Hindley's brother-in-law, David Smith, who had witnessed the murder of one of their victims, 17 year old Edward Evans, at the house Brady and Hindley shared. Evans's axed body was found there and the grisly catalogue of murders unfolded.

The pair had lured children back to their house in Manchester where they had tortured them, taken pictures of them naked, recorded their ordeals on tape, and murdered them before burying their bodies out on nearby moorland.

The remains of 10 year old Lesley Ann Downey and 12 year old John Kilbride were found on Saddleworth Moor, and police continued to search the moor for a further two missing children. No case excited such public revulsion in recent memory, and later appeals for clemency were turned down.

MAY 1

Bye-Bye Beatles, Hello Stones

The annual *New Musical Express* Pollwinners Concert was held at London's Empire Pool, Wembley, this evening, and while lead attractions on the star-studded bill included The Who and The Rolling Stones - the latter, No 1 hit-makers this month with *Paint It Black* - the event was most noteworthy for being the last time The Beatles ever performed before a British audience.

The Stones' astute manager, Andrew Oldham, stole everyone's thunder by announcing that the group would all be starring in a new film, *Only Lovers Left Alive*, to be filmed in August. According to Oldham, a former assistant to The Beatles' press agent, while the Stones would be appearing in individual roles, the group would also be contributing the soundtrack.

Like much of what Oldham promised, *Only Lovers Left Alive* would never be made, remaining just one more of his successful public relations stunts.

MAY 28

Percy Opens Heart But Loses Fortune!

Percy Sledge, an unknown singer from Alabama, today hit No 1 in the US with *When A Man Loves A Woman* – yet could have been forgiven for crying all the way to the bank!

The soulful crooner was a member of The Esquires when he improvised the song's heartfelt lyric, but, in a fit of generosity, he gifted all the writing royalties to two of his bandmates, bassist Cameron Lewis and organist Arthur Wright, who'd come up with the distinctive chord sequence.

Sledge missed out on a fortune in writer's royalties and, to make matters worse, gained nothing when the song topped the US chart a second time in November 1991 when it was recorded by Michael Bolton. In between times, Levi Strauss adopted it as the theme for one of their advertisements. Happily, Sledge's own career continued successfully into the 1990s.

UK TOP 10 SINGLES

1: Pretty Flamingo
- Manfred Mann

2: Sloop John B
- The Beach Boys

3: Daydream
- The Lovin' Spoonful

4: You Don't Have To Say You Love Me
- Dusty Springfield

5: Pied Piper
- Crispian St Peter

6: Bang Bang (My Baby Shot Me Down)
- Cher

7: Wild Thing
- The Troggs

8: Shotgun Wedding
- Roy C

9: Hold Tight
- Dave Dee, Dozy, Beaky, Mick & Tich

10: Sorrow
- The Merseys

MAY 5

Dortmund Spoil Shankly's Season

Having finished the domestic season six points clear of nearest rivals Leeds United, it was assumed that Bill Shankly's all-conquering Liverpool team would make the journey back from Glasgow's Hampden Park with the European Cup Winners' Cup tonight.

Germany's Borussia Dortmund had other ideas, however, and clinched the trophy in front of 41,657 people with a 2-1 win after extra time. Borussia, who had beaten holders West Ham in the semi-final, took the prize with a 40-yard spectacular from winger Libuda, who lobbed keeper Tommy Lawrence's punch back into the Liverpool net.

ARRIVALS
Born this month:
14: Fab Morvan, US pop star (Milli Vanilli)
16: Janet Jackson, US pop superstar
24: Eric Cantona, French international football star, poet
26: Helena Bonham-Carter, UK film and stage actress
30: Helen Sharman, UK astronaut, scientist
31: Johnny Diesel, UK rock guitarist, songwriter.

DEPARTURES
Died this month:
17: Randolph Turpin, UK boxer, World Middleweight Champion 1951, aged 37
(see Came & Went pages)

MAY 21

Clay Beats Cooper To Retain World Crown

AMERICAN BOXER Cassius Clay retained his world heavyweight title in London tonight when he defeated British challenger Henry Cooper in the sixth round of their fight, so ending Cooper's dream of repeating his 1963 knock-down of Clay.

On that occasion, only the end-of-round bell had saved the Kentucky born former Olympic light-heavyweight champion from disaster, and a halt to his progress to the heavyweight title in 1964, when he out ran, out punched and outwitted Sonny Liston.

Clay - about to convert to Islam and become Muhammad Ali - had managed to win that fight by exposing Cooper's tendency to cut badly. He did the same on this occasion, and the referee had no option but to stop the fight when it was obvious that a cut over his left eye had rendered Cooper incapable of seeing the champion.

MAY 23

Seamen's Strike Bites Britain

Ports around Britain were brought to a virtual standstill today while seamen's union leaders met with employers to hammer out a new agreement over overtime payments. Until now, the seamen had worked a 56-hour week with no overtime payments and the unions wanted this reduced to a standard 40 hours. The current deadlock in negotiations resulted in the government declaring a state of emergency to ensure that essential services were maintained. Three days later, Prime Minister Harold Wilson would announce his intention of setting up an independent inquiry into the composition of strike committees which, he believed, were too strongly influenced by left-wingers.

The Sound Of Money?

It was announced this month that *The Sound Of Music*, which won five Oscars - including those for Best Picture and Best Director - at last month's Academy Awards, had also overtaken the 1939 classic *Gone With The Wind* as the highest-grossing movie of all time. Its first year of release had seen it bring more than of $120 million, $70 million from US cinema receipts alone.

In one stroke, the Rodgers and Hammerstein musical starring Julie Andrews solved 20th Century Fox's financial problems, which mostly stemmed from *Cleopatra*, the incredibly expensive (and financially unrewarding) 1963 Taylor-Burton epic whose losses had forced the studio to sell off part of its land for office development.

MAY 30

Hill Wins Indy 500

The British motor racing contingent was much in evidence as the cars lined up for the start of America's greatest road race, the Indianapolis 500, today. Jackie Stewart was leading, with just eight laps to go, when he was forced to pull out of the race, leaving his Scottish compatriot, Jim Clark, (pictured at the wheel of a toy tractor, being pushed by Graham Hill and his son, Damon) and Englishman Hill to fight it out to the finish.

The day - and the title - belonged to Graham Hill and his Lotus-Ford, which averaged 144.3 mph to win the 50th Indy 500.

Jackie Stewart would fare better on May 22 when he emerged victorious in the Monaco Grand Prix, to end a month which had seen the Union Jack lifted on May 1 when England's John Surtees won the Syracuse Grand Prix in Sicily.

Alf Garnett Goes On Air

Today's inaugural screening of *Till Death Us Do Part*, a deliberately controversial British television situation comedy, caused even more of an uproar than writer Johnny Speight intended, or could have hoped. Its impact - and status as a show everyone had to watch - would be reinforced two days later when the Conservatives asked for sight of the script in which their leader, Edward Heath, had been called 'a grammar-school twit'. In a show of political balance, Speight's monstrous creation, the bigoted Alf Garnett, was every bit as scathing about Labour leader Harold Wilson, as well as targeting immigrants, Catholics and others. Not everyone saw the joke, but the show and its catch-phrases – 'Scouse git' and 'silly old moo' among them – became ingrained in the nation's psyche, as well as inspiring an equally successful US counterpart in Archie Bunker and *All In The Family*.

Roy Orbison's Wife In Motor-Cycle Tragedy

Claudette Orbison, wife of US pop star Roy, was killed in a motor-cycle crash today near the couple's home in Nashville. Orbison, who witnessed the crash, had immortalized his wife - then his teenaged sweetheart - with the song *Claudette*, a 1958 hit for The Everly Brothers. This would not be the last time tragedy would hit the man who specialized in dramatic, often heart-rending songs. In September 1968, two of his three children would perish in a fire that consumed his Nashville home while Orbison was on tour in Britain.

OBE For Style-Maker Quant

English fashion designer Mary Quant, who did so much to introduce youth culture to the high street, was awarded the Order of the British Empire (OBE) today, in the Queen's Birthday Honours List. Trained at London's Goldsmith's College, Quant opened her first fashion boutique, *Bazaar*, in Chelsea in 1955, but made what was perhaps her main contribution to an international shift in youth style with her introduction, in 1964, of the miniskirt – a fashion item which virtually came to define the Swinging Sixties. Quant's original use of colour and geometric design were a major influence on 1960s fashion which helped put Britain in the forefront of popular style.

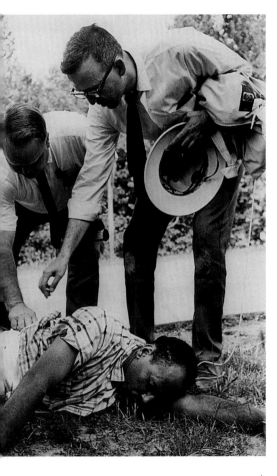

Civil Rights Champ Meredith Shot By Whites

AMERICAN CIVIL RIGHTS activist James Meredith, who became the first black person to break the colour barrier at the University of Mississippi in 1962, was shot in the back today while taking part in a protest march in Mississippi.

Meredith - whose arrival at the University was marked by rioting and confrontation, which resulted in two deaths - was peppered with shot in the neck, shoulders and back shortly after the march crossed the Mississippi state line. A white man was taken into custody by police.

Dr Martin Luther King subsequently took over leadership of the 225-mile march, which Meredith courageously rejoined nineteen days later after hospital treatment for his wounds. 'The day for the negro man being a coward is over', Meredith was reported as saying.

UK TOP 10 SINGLES

1: Strangers In The Night
- Frank Sinatra
2: Monday Monday
- The Mamas & The Papas
3: Sorrow
- The Merseys
4: Paint It, Black
- The Rolling Stones
5: When A Man Loves A Woman
- Percy Sledge
6: Wild Thing
- The Troggs
7: Don't Bring Me Down
- The Animals
8: Promises
- Ken Dodd
9: Sloop John B
- The Beach Boys
10: Paperback Writer
- The Beatles

ARRIVALS
Born this month:
8: Doris May Pearson, UK pop singer (5 Star)
10: David Platt, England international football star, captain

DEPARTURES
Died this month:
7: Jean Hans Arp, French painter, engraver, sculptor, poet, aged 78

JUNE 21

Sick Stones Go To Law

The Rolling Stones prepared for their third US tour in unusual fashion today by suing 14 New York City hotels which had banned the group members from their premises. The suit claimed that the ban damaged The Stones' reputation, as well as violating New York State civil rights laws by 'discriminating on account of national origin'.

Their tour remained on, despite the collapse two weeks earlier of lead singer Mick Jagger. The group's frontman was hospitalized after lengthy tours of Australia and Europe had apparently sapped his strength.

JUNE 7

Reagan Nominated For California Governorship

Just two years after he made his last feature film – Don Siegel's *The Killers* – movie star Ronald Reagan (pictured with wife Nancy) succeeded in winning the Republican Party's nomination for Governor of California today, apparently having been persuaded to run for office by his business friends.

Although he had played a major role in the presidential campaign of Senator Barry Goldwater in 1964, Reagan's swift progress up the Republican Party ladder was something of a surprise – his early political leanings were to the Democratic Party and included a spell as a fiercely liberal leader of the Actors' Union in the 1950s, when he dared to confront the witch-hunting Senate Un-American Activities Committee of Senator Joe McCarthy.

Now more conservative in his beliefs and public image, Reagan had only joined the Republicans four years earlier.

JUNE 16

Cliff's Secret Is Out

US evangelist Billy Graham's Crusade at London's Earls Court hit the headlines today when British pop star Cliff Richard was among those to take the stage and announce that he had accepted Christ. He also treated the assembled 25,000 crowd to a song, appropriately titled *It's No Secret*.

Cliff, who had started his career as a leather-clad rock 'n' roll rebel whose manner appalled parents, also announced that when his Christmas pantomime commitments had finished he would embark on a three-year divinity course, giving up show business completely as of April 1967.

He would change his mind about this, continue as a singer (though alternating sacred and secular releases) and receive a knighthood for his charity work in 1995.

The Moon Passes White Glove Test

FEARS THAT THE MOON might be covered in a layer of dust so deep that any landing craft would disappear beneath the surface were dispelled today when Surveyor 1 – Gemini 9's landing module – made a safe landing and remained firmly in sight. Over a hundred photographs taken by Surveyor 1 and sent back to NASA control in Houston, Texas, had correctly suggested that the surface of the moon would support a manned landing.

Today's success was especially cheering for NASA scientists who had estimated that another three missions would be needed to achieve the first 'soft' landing on the moon's surface. The official view was that the Surveyor programme had leapt ahead by a full year – good news for the budget.

It was also good news for the US regarding its position in the race against the Soviet Union to land a manned craft. The Soviet space agency had appeared to steal a march on NASA by landing a craft similar to Surveyor on the moon four months earlier.

RECORDS TUMBLE AS RYUN GETS GOING

With most of the world's media heading, naturally enough, for England and the mouth-watering prospect of the football World Cup, there was scant international attention paid to the athletics meeting which took place in Berkeley, California, on July 17. Which was a shame, because Jim Ryun was just about to run himself into history for the second of a memorable three times this year.

Already a record-holder by having become - at only 17 - the youngest-ever sub four-minute miler in the world two years earlier, the gangling Kansas-born youngster had begun the season by setting a new world 800m record of 1:44.9.

The Berkeley meet was a hastily arranged replacement for a US-Poland match cancelled amid controversy over Vietnam, but Ryun's preparation was superb - as was his performance in the mile. He powered himself through an electrifying last lap to shatter Michael Jazy's year old record by 2.3 seconds, completing those four laps of the track in 3 mins 51.3 seconds.

Ryun's third achievement of the season came when he set a new US record of 8:25.2 for the two miles. Justly, at the year's end, Jim Ryun was the recipient of the United States' most prestigious sports prize, the Sullivan Award.

Although Ryun would win his third successive US mile title in 1967 with an even better 3:51.1 (achieved with a devastating 52.5 seconds last lap) and, only two weeks later, take an astonishing 2.5 seconds off Herb Elliott's seven-year 1500m world record with 3:33.1, his departure from form and major competitions was just as surprising.

For a few months this year, however, Jim Ryun was the best there was in the world.

NO RECORD, BUT NICKLAUS HOLDS ON TO US MASTERS

It was asking a bit too much to expect Jack Nicklaus to repeat or equal the record-breaking 271 which gave him his second US Masters green jacket in 1965, but in Augusta this April his 288 was enough to win him a full round play-off against Gay Brewer and Tommy Jacobs. In the event, the inevitable was only delayed as Nicklaus' 70 saw off Jacobs by two strokes, while Brewer took a miserable 78 to end up third. But the Nicklaus victory was notable for being only the first time the US Masters had been won in successive years, making that winner's jacket an even more treasured trophy for the 26 year old from Ohio who'd only turned professional in 1962.

He'd also won what would be the first of three British Open titles at Muirfield, with a last-hole birdie which beat the 283 target set by David Thomas and Doug Sanders. But his strong competitive streak lost him not a few British fans in his World Matchplay contest against South African Gary Player.

Hooking a shot on the ninth hole at Wentworth, Nicklaus found himself in a ditch and accepted a penalty drop, but then asked for a free drop as an advertising hoarding was, he said, in line with the hole. The referee, former British Walker Cup captain Colonel Tony Duncan, refused and offered to withdraw when Nicklaus accused him of making 'a bum decision'.

When Duncan again offered to hand over to someone else on the next tee, and Nicklaus agreed, the general consensus - when Player won the game 6 & 4 - was that justice had been done to cancel out the American's pretty unsportsmanlike behaviour.

BRABHAM SCORES D-I-Y WORLD CHAMPIONSHIP VICTORY

With the Grand Prix racing season thrown into confusion by the introduction of a 3-litre formula, and teams turning to some weird and wonderful configurations of horsepower, it was Jack Brabham who emerged as the Formula One champion - the only driver ever to win the title with a car bearing his own name as constructor.

Brabham - the Australian speedway champ with engineering training, who'd moved to Britain in 1955 to begin a world championship career which would give him 14 Grand Prix wins out of 126 starts - had introduced the Brabham car in 1962 after teaming up with designer Ron Tauranac.

The 1966 Brabham-Repco (sponsored by the Australian spare parts distributor, Repco) boasted an alloy V-8 Oldsmobile engine block with added alloy heads, overhead camshafts and fuel injection. It helped Brabham - a ferocious and canny competitor - to win four races to take both his third World Championship and the Constructors' Championship, a unique double. It is likely to remain so, given the multi-billion investment game Formula One racing has become in recent years.

A reclusive man, 'Black' Jack Brabham would be awarded the OBE this year, and knighted in 1979. All three of his sons - Gary, David and Geoff - would become racing drivers, although none would be able to emulate their illustrious father.

Jack Nicklaus

JULY 19

Sinatra Marries Mia

Frank Sinatra, (pictured centre) the singer with the silver tongue, today married young film actress Mia Farrow (near left) in a ceremony at Las Vegas in Nevada. The 51 year old crooner, one of the best-selling pop artists of the 1940s, 1950s and 1960s, had been married twice before, his last marriage being to the very glamorous Ava Gardner.

Showbiz cynics had been heard to suggest his decision to marry the much younger Mia, daughter of film director John Farrow and actress Maureen O'Sullivan, was summed up in the title of the hit single he'd recently scored with his daughter, Nancy - *Something Stupid*.

The new Mrs Sinatra was already a star of TV's *Peyton Place*, but would be best known for her part in 1968's *Rosemary's Baby* before her celebrated - and ultimately messy - relationship with Woody Allen. It was clearly a popular month for movie marriages: five days earlier, French screen star Brigitte Bardot had married millionaire Gunther Sachs.

Race Riots Rock US Cities

UNEMPLOYMENT AND DEPRIVATION among the poor populations of America's inner-city ghettos were cited as the main causes of the race riots which raged through much of July, leaving a trail of destruction, death and recrimination on all sides.

Whites and blacks fought police in Chicago, Cleveland and New York, leaving many injured. Fire-bomb and sniper attacks were made on police officers, and more than 4,000 National Guardsmen were called in to support police in Chicago today in a grim finale.

The fatal shooting, by police, of a black mother and the wounding of her three children, set off a new wave of rioting in Cleveland, where two people had already died and more than 50 people had been injured after a civil rights march through an all-white neighbourhood degenerated into street-fighting.

In New York, the fighting had a different slant, being confined mainly to a week of running battles between rival gangs of Puerto Ricans, blacks and whites which left at least two dead. Gang leaders ignored a call by Mayor John Lindsay for them to settle their differences around a conference table.

UK Wage Freeze Causes Casualties

George Brown, Britain's Secretary of State for Economic Affairs, today tendered his resignation over the current economic crisis. Prime Minister Harold Wilson had said it was time to halt the inflation which was running away with the economy, and since the resignation of Frank Cousins from his cabinet post as Minister of Technology three weeks ago, the cabinet had been split over how to handle the current economic crisis.

Cousins, a former union leader, had opposed the strict measures which the PM announced today – a six-month wage freeze followed by a six-month period of tight restraint, and a further 12-month freeze on price increases. Despite his opposition, the Trade Union Congress general council voted to back the Government's wage freeze policy. Brown, who had been persuaded to withdraw his resignation, would move to the Foreign Office in an August reshuffle.

Welsh Nationalist MP Joins Commons

Plaid Cymru, the Welsh nationalist party, celebrated today as Gwynfor Evans, victor in a recent Carmarthen by-election, was sworn in as their first representative in the British parliament. Expected to refuse to take the oath of allegiance in English, the Welsh-speaking Evans didn't buck the system. But his request to take the oath again in his native tongue was refused firmly by the Speaker - no one else would know what he was saying!

UK TOP 10 SINGLES

1: Sunny Afternoon
- The Kinks

2: River Deep Mountain High
- Ike & Tina Turner

3: Nobody Needs Your Love
- Gene Pitney

4: Get Away
- Georgie Fame

5: Strangers In The Night
- Frank Sinatra

6: Bus Stop
- The Hollies

7: Paperback Writer
- The Beatles

8: Out Of Time
- Chris Farlowe

9: Black Is Black
- Los Bravos

10: Hideaway
- Dave Dee, Dozy, Beaky, Mick & Tich

JULY 30

England Win Football's World Cup

MAKING FULL USE OF THEIR home advantage, the England football team today won the game's ultimate prize - the Jules Rimet Trophy, or World Cup - with a 4-2 victory over West Germany at Wembley Stadium. Hero of the hour was striker Geoff Hurst, whose hat trick put the result beyond doubt after Wolfgang Weber had levelled the scores at 2-2 with a last-gasp goal and forced the game into extra time.

The third goal, the first in that added period, was a controversial one. Hurst's shot bounced down off the crossbar and was adjudged to have crossed the line by Russian linesman, Mr Backharamov, despite German protests that it hadn't.

A fourth goal - Hurst's third, with Martin Peters having scored England's second - made the game safe in the last seconds as English supporters started to encroach upon the pitch in premature celebration. That became unbridled hysteria when England captain Bobby Moore accepted the gold trophy from the Queen.

Manager Alf Ramsey received a knighthood for masterminding the successful campaign, but England were to perish at the quarter-final stage against the same opposition in Mexico when attempting to retain the trophy in 1970.

JULY 23

Sad Death Of Clift, Tortured Star

The film world lost one of its most gifted actors today when Montgomery Clift suffered a fatal heart attack at the relatively young age of 45. Behind Clift's early demise lay a life of sustained drug and alcohol abuse caused by the pressure of concealing his homosexuality and his very real difficulty in handling the stardom part of acting success.

Nominated for an Academy Award in his 1948 début *The Search*, and again in 1953 for *From Here To Eternity*, he was able - like Rock Hudson - to submerge his real inclinations to become a leading romantic actor. The cost, however, proved too great, and he paid it in full today.

JULY 29

Dylan Crashes Bike, Drops Out

Influential folk-rock star Bob Dylan crashed his Triumph 55 motor-cycle near his home in Woodstock, New York State, today. The accident left him with unspecified injuries, apparently including broken neck vertebrae, and forced an 18-month period of recuperation and seclusion during which he would record the legendary *Basement Tapes* with his backing group, The Band. Meanwhile, his record label, Columbia/CBS, would continue with the scheduled release, weeks later, of his double album *Blonde On Blonde*.

Recorded in the first three months of the year, it contained such classics as *Just Like A Woman* and *Absolutely Sweet Marie*. One entire side of the album, which reached No 9 in the States and No 3 in Britain, was devoted to a single song, *Sad Eyed Lady Of The Lowlands*.

AUG

London Police Deaths Spark Huge Manhunt

A MAJOR NATIONWIDE MANHUNT was launched by Scotland Yard tonight after three London policemen were shot dead by men whose car they were trailing near Wormwood Scrubs prison. The killers jumped from their vehicle and shot two of the detectives when they approached, shooting the third officer as he sat behind the steering-wheel.

The three officers were 30 year old Christopher Head, 25 year old David Wombwell, and the 41 year old driver, Geoffrey Fox. Although he did not have time to radio for help, he did scribble the registration number of the killers' car before he died.

Working on the theory that the three had stumbled on a jailbreak plot, their colleagues would arrest two men within a week - one in London, the other in Glasgow. Both would be found guilty of the killings and sentenced to life terms.

Indonesian Bush War Ends

Hostilities between Malaysia and Indonesia, which had continued unbroken for the past three years, finally ended today when a peace treaty was signed in Djakarta to 'normalize' relations between the Asian neighbours.

The bush war had been caused by Indonesia's President Sukarno's refusal to acknowledge the right of former British colonies Sabah and Sarawak to become part of Malaysia, and his attempt to expel British troops from the region.

His authority weakened by an attempted coup last October, Sukarno's position had worsened in the past few weeks when Indonesian military leaders - who'd saved him last year - were discovered to be having secret peace talks with Malaysia's government. Weary of a war which was draining their country's slender resources, they had also tired of Sukarno's continued anti-imperialistic fixation.

Today's agreement also ended Sukarno's attempts to expel British forces which had supported Malaysia's claim to the disputed territory.

Drug Overdose Kills US Comic Lenny Bruce

Lenny Bruce (pictured), the American comedian who, for the previous ten years, had delighted US nightclub audiences with his risqué satire, died today of a heroin overdose at the age of 39. It's strange but true that his use of 'dirty words' attracted the attention of the United States Government which - clearly worried by what they saw as a subversive influence - subjected him to FBI harassment that saw him arrested and imprisoned on obscenity charges in 1961. Bruce's stand-up comedy act, which covered such no-go areas as sexual fantasies, racial prejudice and religious tensions, didn't just get the thumbs-down from US authorities - he was also banned in Britain and Australia. A legend among his peers, Bruce's legacy was as a major influence on the work of a new wave of alternative comedians that would follow in the 1980s.

Beatles' Stateside Farewell

The Beatles' last ever tour - and their fourth of the United States - began today at Chicago's Universal Amphitheatre, where they topped a bill comprising The Cyrcle, The Ronettes, The Remains and Bobby Hebb. Public interest was so intense that the three leading US TV networks had all shown the band's press conference at the Astor Towers Hotel, Chicago, shortly after their arrival.

The tour would continue with a riotous sell-out show before 100,000 screaming fans at New York's Shea Stadium on August 23. The final concert, at San Francisco's Candlestick Park on August 29, ended, not with one of The Beatles' many million-selling classics, but with their version of Little Richard's *Long Tall Sally*.

UK TOP 10 SINGLES

1: With A Girl Like You
- The Troggs
2: Black Is Black
- Los Bravos
3: The More I See You
- Chris Montez
4: Mama
- Dave Berry
5: God Only Knows
- The Beach Boys
6: Out Of Time
- Chris Farlowe
7: Yellow Submarine/Eleanor Rigby
- The Beatles
8: Visions
- Cliff Richard
9: Summer In The City
- The Lovin' Spoonful
10: Love Letters
- Elvis Presley

Hawker Harrier Takes Off AUGUST 31

The first pre-production Hawker Harrier, the world's first VTOL (Vertical Take-Off and Landing) warplane, made its maiden flight today, shortly before it was shown to the public at the Farnborough Air Show.

Along with Concorde, the Harrier would prove the British aviation success story of its generation. The US armed services would order it in quantity, while it would prove instrumental in settling the Falklands War in 1982 while

operating from the Royal Navy's aircraft-carriers.

Its ability to change from normal flight to hovering mode - known as VIFF or Vector in Forward Flight - gave it a manoeuvrability no other aircraft could match.

AUGUST 30

Mao's 'Little Red Book' A Licence To Destroy

FOR THE THOUSANDS OF communist students who formed China's Red Guard, the only book worth reading was the *Little Red Book*, which contained quotations from the works of Chairman Mao Tse-tung. Students country-wide - their universities shut and their professors paraded in the streets wearing dunces' caps - paralysed entire cities this month as they organized large demonstrations in which the book and pictures of Mao took pride of place.

Anything old or foreign was denounced or destroyed, while Mao's exhortation, first made in 1927, that 'a revolution is an insurrection, an act of violence by which one class overthrows another' vied with 'Soviet revisionism and US imperialism' for the slogan of the month title.

The Chinese Government showed an equally aggressive anti-West stance today in the capital, Beijing, when it promised more aid for the North Vietnamese communist forces in their fight against US-backed South Vietnam.

AUGUST 26

Germany Counts Cost Of 'Widowmaker'

The crash of the sixtieth Luftwaffe US-built Lockheed Starfighter jet to be destroyed in training flights led to a crisis which was made public for the first time today when the Inspector-General of the West German Air Force, Werner Panitzki, gave a newspaper interview.

Resignations by senior officers in the West German Ministry of Defence followed as public disquiet about the losses in men and aircraft grew. Panitzki paid for his candour with a long suspension and a reprimand. Eventually, however, loss rates were reduced as Luftwaffe pilots grew in experience and ground crews learned how to maintain the aircraft which had been given the macabre nickname of 'the widowmaker'.

AUGUST 20

Arsenal Turn To Physio Mee

After sacking soccer legend Billy Wright as manager at the end of the previous season, leading London soccer club Arsenal put their faith in former physiotherapist Bertie Mee to put the club back on the road to glory this month. Wright's unsuccessful four-year reign had failed to put silverware in Highbury's marble halls – bare since their Championship victory in 1953 – and appointing the untried 46 year old Mee was 'a surprise, but a very pleasant one' to the man himself.

Nevertheless, Mee, who had worked with the players for six years behind the scenes, would prove highly successful – and he made his first master stroke by luring coach Dave Sexton from Fulham to work with him. Within four years, the League and Cup double would be within his grasp.

39

Winwood Wins 'White Soul' Contest By Miles

No one ever disputed that most British groups owed a huge debt to US originators of the various strands of popular music, whether we're talking rock 'n' roll, country or R&B. And it was that last music form, exemplified by the productions of Atlantic and Motown especially, which had many a white Brit straining his (and sometimes her) tonsils to sound as soulful as Ray Charles, say, or Marvin Gaye, Aretha Franklin or Diana Ross.

Many did a decent job, but the arrival of The Spencer Davis Group in 1964 had delivered the undisputed best white soul singer in Britain in the precocious form of the 16 year old Steve Winwood who, with his bassist brother Muff and drummer Peter York, helped the band's nominal guitar-playing leader create some superb music.

After scoring middling hits in 1964 and 1965, The Spencer Davis Group - with Steve's excellent organ playing and unique voice well to the fore - finally broke through to the big time in late 1965 with their No 1 *Keep On Running.*

This year would see them build on that with their March No 1 S*omebody Help Me,* and their No 2 *Gimme Some Loving* in November, between which they slotted the Top 20 hit *When I Come Home.*

Strangely, it would not be until 1967 - when Steve Winwood was busy forming his influential psychedelic band, Traffic - that The Spencer Davis Group's singles began taking off in the United States, where *Gimme Some Loving* and *I'm A Man* finally gave the Wolverhampton-area group decent chart positions.

After many years of reinforcing his brilliance with various versions of Traffic, and a brief spell with Blind Faith, Winwood would reappear in the electronic keyboard 1980s to become one of the world's most successful solo recording acts, that voice still intact, and still capable of raising the hairs on the back of your neck.

DUSTY TAKES TO THE TELLY

Top British pop singer Dusty Springfield proved that she was much more than just a beehive hairdo and a pretty face in August this year by hosting her own British television series.

The former lead singer of folk trio The Springfields (who'd scored in 1962 and '63 with *Island Of Dreams,* Say *I Won't Be There* and *Come On Home*) spread her solo wings in the company of guests like Spanish-American José Feliciano and Welsh sex symbol Tom Jones, with Lesley Duncan and future Blue Mink star Madeline Bell among the resident backing vocalists.

Dusty, who'd been born Mary O'Brien, had proved an instant international hit with her big soulful voice and productions which owed everything to the sounds coming out of Motown. Her biggest past successes had come via *I Only Want To Be With You, I Just Don't Know What To Do With Myself* and *In The Middle Of Nowhere,* but they'd all be eclipsed by her first UK No 1, *You Don't Have To Say You Love Me,* in March this year.

Strangely, only one of her UK hits - *I Only Want To Be With You* - had been promoted well enough in the US to score there, and Dusty would eventually insist on a release from her American contract, a move to the more sympathetic Atlantic label, and the same studio team who worked with the likes of Aretha Franklin.

For now, Dusty's TV series proved so popular it would be brought back for a second series in August 1967.

BOOS FOR ELECTRIC DYLAN

Although folk-protest singer and songwriter Bob Dylan had long since begun using electric instrumentation on his hugely successful albums (in May last year he'd had no fewer than four albums in the UK Top 20, with *Bringing It All Back Home* displacing *Beatles For Sale* as Britain's No 1), this year's British and European tour with a full electric band (The Band, in fact) was the cue for purists to express their displeasure loudly.

With his *Highway 61 Revisited* album still riding high on both sides of the Atlantic and the rollicking *Rainy Day Women #12 & 35* lodged at No 2 in the US at the beginning of May, Dylan's 14-day Irish and British tour was marred by the sound of boos, catcalls and the sound of departing feet once he and The Band cranked up.

On May 26, at London's Royal Albert Hall, the tour ended with much more of the same and the young man born Robert Zimmerman left Britain less than gruntled. The moaning minority would be proved out of step in August when Dylan's double album, *Blonde On Blonde*, would become Britain's No 3 LP in its first week on sale.

Sadly, by that time Dylan was receiving treatment for broken neck vertebrae after crashing his motor-bike near his home in Woodstock. It would be almost two years before he'd return to the concert stage.

Dusty Springfield

SEPTEMBER 6

Apartheid Architect Verwoerd Assassinated

DR HENDRIK VERWOERD (pictured) - one of the men who helped create South Africa's racist apartheid laws, and enforced them as the nation's premier for eight years - was stabbed to death in the House of Assembly today. His assassin was a messenger working in the country's parliament buildings who, colleagues said, was always talking about guns and quoting the Bible.

Verwoerd, who had survived a previous attempt on his life six years earlier, was stabbed four times in the chest with a long stiletto blade which the messenger, Demetrio Tsafendas, pulled from his belt. Although it was obvious that the Prime Minister, who was 64, had been fatally wounded, he was rushed to a nearby hospital where doctors pronounced him dead.

Appointed Minister of Native Affairs in 1950, Verwoerd played an active role in creating the rules, regulations and increasingly strict laws aimed at keeping South Africa's whites, blacks and those of mixed-race (the so-called Cape Coloureds) strictly segregated in every way. An unreconstructed hard-liner and white supremacist, it was he who set up the Bantu homelands in the 1950s, moving thousands of people into scrubland often incapable of sustaining agriculture - a move matched only by Hitler's Final Solution or Stalin's gulags. Ironically, it was not his harsh apartheid line his assassin said had prompted his actions. Tsafendas thought Verwoerd was 'doing too much for the coloureds, and nothing for the poor whites'.

SEPTEMBER 16

Gemini 11 Splashes Down

US astronauts Charles Conrad and Richard Gordon, who set a new altitude record of 850 miles on their recent space mission, today returned safely to earth in their Gemini 11 capsule. Conrad described the view from 850 miles up as 'fantastic'.

The Gemini 11 mission made 44 orbits of the earth during its 71-hour journey and achieved a successful docking with the companion Agena spacecraft to which it remained tied by a 100-foot line. The manoeuvre proved that spacecraft could orbit in formation relatively easily, which was good news for NASA's projected lunar landings.

SEPTEMBER 6

Birth Control Pill Pioneer Sanger Dies

Margaret Sanger, the American pioneer of birth control, who saw the possibilities of the contraceptive pill and launched a campaign urging scientists to make the dream a reality, died today at the age of 82. The daughter of a woman exhausted by constant childbearing, and who worked as a nurse, she was all too familiar with the botched abortions and huge families which were a result of the lack of birth control.

A pupil of British psychologist Havelock Ellis, Sanger shared the establishment's victimization of her mentor. In 1915, she was arrested for sending birth control literature through the US Mail and suffered a similar fate shortly afterwards when she opened a clinic in Brooklyn, New York. As the idea of birth control gained wider acceptability, Sanger remained at the forefront of the campaign, becoming the first president of both the US National Committee on Federal Legislation for Birth Control, in 1923, and the International Planned Parenthood Foundation 30 years later.

SEPTEMBER 5

Lennon Enlists For Lester

John Lennon, best known for his work as singer and songwriter with The Beatles, today flew to Germany where he was to begin filming How I Won The War, his first straight movie role (and the first without his fellow musicians). His part was the unlikely named Private Gripweed.

Richard Lester, who had worked with The Beatles on A Hard Day's Night and Help, was director, and the film received excellent notices, not only for Lennon's Goon-like responses to the chaos around him, but also for the excellent performances of Michael Crawford and Roy Kinnear.

Paul McCartney, in contrast, preferred to confine his dabbling in 'serious' cinema to composing the score for the Hayley Mills/Hywel Bennett film The Family Way, which would be premièred in December.

DEPARTURES

Died this month:

6: Dr Hendrik Frensch Verwoerd, South African leader, PM 1958-66 *(see main story)*; Margaret Sanger, US birth control pioneer *(see main story)*

21: Paul Reynaud, French politician, aged 88

25: 'Billy' Smart (William George Smart), British circus-owner, showman, aged 73

28: André Breton, French poet, author, surrealist *(see main story)*

Monkee Mania Hits US

SEPTEMBER 12

American television today welcomed a new sensation – The Monkees (pictured), a four-man pop group specifically formed by pop mogul Don Kirshner to play in a TV series about their strictly scripted exploits.

As pop history would soon prove, truth could become stranger than fiction. The universally attractive features of Davy Jones, Mike Nesmith, Micky Dolenz and Peter Tork – future superstar Stephen Stills was allegedly rejected during screen tests for having crooked teeth – became an instant hit with teens and twenties, and their first single, *Last Train To Clarksville*, would race to No 1 in the US charts in November.

They would tour (with Jimi Hendrix, unbelievably, as support) and even - horror of horrors - write their own songs and play their own instruments before disbanding.

Baez Goes Back To School

Joan Baez, the folk-singer whose version of *We Shall Overcome* became the anthem of US civil rights protesters earlier this decade, took direct action when she led a group of black children to an all-white school in Mississippi to protest against segregation in the southern state.

Dr Martin Luther King Jr, the civil rights leader, had focused on the town of Grenada, where almost 50 per cent of the population was black, to highlight the injustices of Mississippi's policies. Last week, police looked on passively as a white mob attacked a group of blacks who were trying to integrate a school in the town.

Brabham Wins Grand Prix In 'Home-Made' Car!

AUSTRALIAN RACING driver Jack Brabham won the Italian Grand Prix at Monza today and, in the process, took the World Drivers' Championship for the third time.

Nothing remarkable about that - winning races was something Brabham did a lot during his victory-rich career. But today's win was especially impressive because Brabham did not, like his competitors, drive a machine built and maintained by a team from one of the world's leading motor companies, but a vehicle of his own design - the Repco-Brabham.

Brabham, who was 40 this year, was trained as an engineer and began his motor-racing career after World War II in 'midget' cars. He was no stranger to the concept of 'self-help', having won the championship for the first time in 1959 by clambering out of the driving-seat of his Cooper-Climax and pushing the car over the finishing line at Sebring, the Florida racetrack!

Father Of Surrealism Dies

The French poet André Breton, creator of the Surrealist movement which had such a profound influence on art in the twentieth century, died today at the age of 70. Breton published his first *Surrealist Manifesto* in 1924, a work in which he proposed the liberation of artistic expression from reason, logic or morals.

But if free uncensored literature from the likes of Aragon, Desnos and Eluard was where surrealism was born, it was in the visual arts that it made its biggest impression, with painters such as Salvador Dali, René Magritte and Joan Miró achieving widespread public recognition.

Aberfan Loses Its Children In Coal Tip Disaster

ALL OF BRITAIN WAS IN mourning today for the small Welsh mining community of Aberfan, where a two million-ton slag-heap of deposits from the local coal-mine slid down a hillside and demolished the village school, killing 116 children and 28 adults. The school was engulfed within seconds, as were a farmhouse and a row of cottages.

As a full inquiry was ordered into the disaster, British Prime Minister Harold Wilson summed up the feelings of the nation when he said, 'I don't think any of us can find words to describe this tragedy'. Both he and the Duke of Edinburgh visited the disaster scene as rescue workers toiled tirelessly to locate bodies buried under tons of slurry and shale.

The rescuers, many of them desperate parents of children who attended the school, worked all day and throughout the following night, but few were brought out alive - the disaster had almost completely robbed the village of its next generation.

Even as work continued to retrieve bodies, allegations were made that the local authority, Merthyr Tydfil Borough Council, had recently refused to carry out a safety check on the tip. Already there was speculation that a previously undiscovered underground spring may have made the heap unstable.

The children of Aberfan would be buried together in a combined funeral service, their final resting-place made into a permanent memorial and reminder for future generations.

OCTOBER 18

Posthumous Pardon For Timothy Evans

Timothy Evans, the 25 year old truck driver who was convicted and hanged for the murder of his wife and young daughter in 1950, was today granted a free pardon by the Queen after a long campaign to clear his name.

A Home Office inquiry, several debates in the House of Commons and a final review of evidence by a High Court judge, all led to the conclusion that there was insufficient evidence against Evans, who had consistently denied the charges against him.

It was widely believed that Evans's wife and daughter had almost certainly been murdered by their lodger, John Christie, who was himself later convicted and hanged for the murders of several women at their home, the now notorious 10 Rillington Place, in London's Notting Hill district.

OCTOBER 26

LBJ Visits Troops In Vietnam

Secrecy surrounded the arrival in South Vietnam of US President Lyndon Johnson at the Cam Ranh Bay base today. Johnson, who was on a 17-day tour of the South Pacific, broke his journey for an informal, two and a half hour meeting with the GIs on Vietnam's front line.

The visit, carried out in the steamy heat of the war zone, clearly affected the President who in a moving farewell speech to the troops bade them to come home 'safe and sound'. The secrecy built into LBJ's lightning stop was to protect him from the risk of a Vietcong attack on the base.

OCTOBER 1

Albert Speer Released From Spandau

Albert Speer, the German architect whose organizational skills became invaluable to the Nazi Party, was released from Spandau Prison in Berlin today, having served the 20-year sentence meted out to him at the Nuremberg war-crime trials at the end of World War II. Speer played a key role in the design, planning and running of the vast industrial base vital to the Nazi war effort, although in the closing stages of the war he found himself at odds with Hitler and the Nazi philosophy generally. Now aged 61, Speer would retire into a deliberately low-profile obscurity, and die in 1981.

OCTOBER 31

Strike Hits BMC Plants

No Morris or Austin motor cars were made in Britain today as an unofficial strike against a British Motor Corporation (BMC) redundancy plan intensified to close all the company's factories.

The strike - which would not end until October 11, but would continue to rumble on for many months in the shape of local stoppages - followed BMC's announcement that 12,000 of its 109,000 workers were to be laid off in a bid to restore the group to profitability. All 24,000 Austin and Morris car section employees stayed out today.

OCTOBER 18

France Gets First Experience Of Jimi

The Jimi Hendrix Experience, a British-based hard-rock trio led by a black, left-handed guitarist from Seattle, made their world début today – in France! Fans of local rock legend Johnny Halliday, gathered at the Olympia Theatre in Paris, were privileged to observe the first public performance from a band whose short life would change the history of rock music.

On their return to London, the Experience – Hendrix, bass-player Noel Redding and drummer Mitch Mitchell – would play a series of club dates attended by luminaries such as British blues guitarist Eric Clapton, The Who's Pete Townshend and Rolling Stones guitarist Brian Jones. All would rave about the new 'wild man of pop' who would release his first single, *Hey Joe*, in December.

OCTOBER 22

Russians Spring George Blake

IN WHAT COULD HAVE been a chapter from any novel by the likes of Ian Fleming, John Le Carré or Len Deighton, convicted double agent George Blake went missing from his cell at London's Wormwood Scrubs prison (pictured) today and escaped to freedom after scaling an outer wall.

Blake, a former British diplomat who was sentenced to a record 42 years for spying in 1961, made his escape with a home-made rope ladder reinforced with ten pairs of knitting-needles. The only clue police reported finding at the scene was a single pink chrysanthemum, although red might have been more appropriate as British officials believed Blake's escape was probably organized by the KGB.

The 46 year old was imprisoned after admitting he'd passed every document he could to the Russians during the nine years he worked as a diplomat in Germany and Lebanon. He had been captured by North Korean communists while British vice-consul in the South Korean capital of Seoul, and it was thought he'd been brainwashed during his three years in captivity.

Blake would resurface in East Berlin a few weeks later, refusing to say how he'd engineered his Houdini act. That would remain a mystery until the early 1990s when two British anti-nuclear protesters who'd met Blake in prison admitted that they'd helped him.

OCT

'Red Dean' Johnson Dies

The political clergyman who rose to the position of Dean of Canterbury Cathedral at the crowning point of a career in the Church of England, and who had been described as both a 'saint' and a 'commie', died today at the age of 92. Dr Hewlitt Johnson became known as the 'Red Dean' when he spoke out during the Spanish Civil War, about which he said, 'I saw red – you can call me red.'

He spent his early life working in the slums of Manchester and, although he was never a member of the Communist Party, was well known for his support of the Soviet Union, which he visited in the late 1930s. Dr Johnson was vilified for his remark 'If Jesus Christ were alive today he would be a communist'.

MAY 17

RANDOLPH TURPIN: THE TRAGIC CHAMP

The financial and domestic pressures which plagued the last years of Randolph Turpin - the British boxing champion who so memorably became world middleweight champion in July 1951 when he defeated the supposedly untouchable 'Sugar' Ray Robinson - obviously became too much for a remarkably brave man. On this day, he took a gun and shot himself at his home in Leamington Spa, Warwickshire, just a few weeks short of his thirty-eighth birthday.

Rated by many as the most able British boxer since the end of World War II, Turpin was only one of three brothers who excelled at the sport. He first took it up while serving with the Royal Navy, and was only 17 years old when he became the Amateur Boxing Association welterweight champion. Turning professional in 1950, he won the British middleweight title and, in the following year, became European champion by knocking out Dutchman Luc van Dam in a mere 48 seconds!

That put him in line for a crack at 'Sugar' Ray Robinson's world crown, and if the US champ approached their fight in London casually, Turpin didn't and was declared winner on points. His reign would last only two months - in New York, Robinson was well prepared for their return fight which was ended in the tenth round when Turpin endured a ferocious attack from a badly-cut Robinson until the referee stepped in to save him further punishment.

In 1952 Turpin beat Don Cockell to take the British and Commonwealth light-heavyweight titles, and became the Commonwealth middleweight champ later that same year. In 1953 he successfully defended his European middleweight title before he was given another shot at the world middleweight crown. Robinson had briefly retired, and while the rest of the world recognized Turpin as champ, US authorities claimed the title belonged to Carl 'Bobo' Olson.

When they met to settle it, Turpin - already dogged by personal problems - put up a poor showing and was outpointed by Olson. Apart from a few more wins, Turpin was on a slide and he retired in 1958, his considerable earnings already depleted. He tried to revive his fortunes by promoting boxing and wrestling tournaments, but when those failed, Turpin decided enough was enough.

FEBRUARY 20

ADMIRAL CHESTER NIMITZ: HERO OF THE PACIFIC WAR

Although his more dynamic and self-promoting personality would give General Douglas MacArthur the greater historical profile, even he would be the first to acknowledge that the tactical genius and strategic World War II victories of Fleet-Admiral Chester Nimitz, who died today at the age of 81, played as great a part in the defeat of Japan as any.

A career seaman from his teens, in December 1941 Nimitz had risen to become Chief of the US Navy Bureau of Navigation when he was appointed Commander-in-Chief of the US Pacific Fleet, a post he would hold until the war's end in 1945 when he and MacArthur accepted the Japanese surrender on board his flagship, the USS Missouri.

It was Nimitz's initial victory in the 1942 Battle of the Coral Sea which restored US communications with

Randolph Turpin battles with 'Sugar' Ray Robinson in July 1951

Australia, while triumph in the Battle of Midway, in June that year, ensured protection for US bases on Hawaii. In 1943 he successfully attacked Japanese forces at Guadalcanal before beginning a leap-frogging series of assaults on less well-defended islands behind Japanese lines to cut off main the enemy troop concentrations.

In November 1943 Nimitz began the 18-month Central Pacific offensive which would begin at Tarawa and culminate at Iwo Jima and Okinawa in 1945 - a brilliant recovery from the disaster of Japan's surprise attack on Pearl Harbor in 1941 which had left most of the US Pacific fleet in ruins.

Art Treasures Lost As Florence Is Flooded

ALTHOUGH EXPERTS PUT THE value of damage in excess of £60 million ($100m), to many the cost caused by today's flooding in Florence was incalculable, with many historic works of art damaged beyond repair. Winds of up to 90 mph and days of constant rain had caused the Arno River to burst its banks, leaving two-thirds of the northern Italian city submerged under six feet of water.

When the floodwater began to recede several days later, revealing the full extent of the damage, the job of cleaning up the thick sludge commenced. Teams of restoration experts from around the world were called in to help save books, paintings and sculptures in a city which contained a vast wealth of cultural treasures.

Among the most notable casualties were the world-famous Uffizi Gallery, where more than 100,000 photographic negatives of paintings were destroyed, the city's cathedral, where the bronze Door of Paradise was swept away by the flood, and the National Library, where countless thousands of books were damaged by water.

Venice, too, suffered in the storms, which washed away several shops on the city's famous 14th-century *Ponte Vecchio*, the only ancient bridge left standing after World War II.

17 Year Old Twiggy Sets The Scene

The mini-skirt was this year's fashion sensation, and fashion model Twiggy - real name Leslie Hornsby (pictured) - probably did more to popularize the innovation than any other. With her thick eyelashes, short bobbed hair, and apparently endless legs, the skinny 17 year old, who weighed in at just six and a half stone (91 lbs) and earned up to an unprecedented 10 guineas ($25) an hour in modelling fees, personified 'Swinging London' and epitomized the Carnaby Street look. And Carnaby Street, together with Mary Quant's boutique in the Kings Road and Barbara Hulanicki's Biba in Kensington Church Street, was *the* place to shop and be seen in these groovy new styles.

NOVEMBER 16

TV Drama Sparks Homeless Debate

Tonight's screening of Jeremy Sandford's *Cathy Come Home*, a powerful drama in the BBC's Wednesday Play series for new playwrights, caused real-life headlines in Britain this month.

Starring Carol White and Ray Brooks as a young, homeless couple, it had such an impact that it was repeated within two months – an unprecedented accolade –

while the public indignation it roused helped turn the small housing pressure group Shelter into a major charity.

Among the other groundbreaking plays presented in the series was Nell Dunn's gritty *Up The Junction*, while Dennis Potter was among the young writers who would also use the controversial showcase to advantage.

UK TOP 10 SINGLES

1: Reach Out I'll Be There
- The Four Tops
2: Stop! Stop! Stop!
- The Hollies
3: Semi-Detached Suburban Mr Jones
- Manfred Mann
4: High Time
- Paul Jones
5: Good Vibrations
- The Beach Boys
6: I Can't Control Myself
- The Troggs
7: Distant Drums
- Jim Reeves
8: Gimme Some Loving
- The Spencer Davis Group
9: If I Were A Carpenter
- Bobby Darin
10: No Milk Today
- Herman's Hermits

NOVEMBER 1

Vietcong Shell Saigon

Using launch pads constructed from bamboo, the North Vietnamese Vietcong today bombarded the outskirts of the South Vietnamese capital, Saigon, today. It was an audacious attack, made all the more effective because the Vietcong's firing positions were situated on the edge of jungle, into which they were able to vanish by the time US and South Vietnamese troops arrived. The missiles used, Russian-built Katyusha rockets, were said not to be a serious military weapon - but they did succeed in demoralizing Saigon's civilian population as they flew overhead making a distinctive wailing sound.

NOVEMBER 25

Warren Mitchell, known to millions as Alf Garnett in Till Death Us Do Part, *was voted Britain's best TV actor of the year*

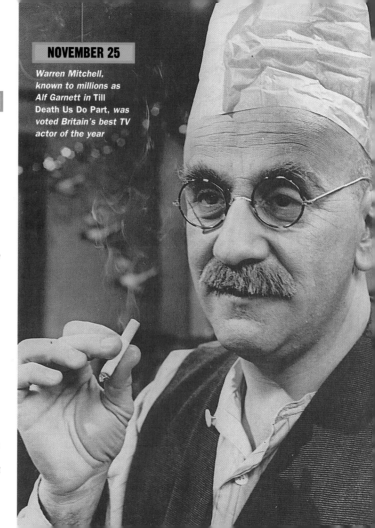

'Buzz' Aldrin Celebrates his first Walk In Space

NASA ASTRONAUT 'BUZZ' ALDRIN made his first space walk - one of the most successful of the Gemini programme - during the twelfth, and last, mission of that project, which returned safely to earth today.

When Dr Edwin Aldrin (to give his full name) joined NASA in 1963 he had already completed a full and active career in the US Air Force, flying over 60 combat missions during the Korean War and spending three years in West Germany flying F-100 jet fighters.

This month's walk was to be one of only two in Aldrin's career. The other, most famously, was during the Apollo 11 mission, when he became the second man to set foot on the surface of the moon.

Aldrin then resigned from space duties to become commanding officer of the Test Pilot School at Edwards Air Force Base in California. However, his open support of civil rights protests while working for NASA caused friction with officialdom and in the early 1970s he suffered a nervous breakdown and retired.

Barbados Gains Independence

The tiny Windward Island nation of Barbados was given its independence by Britain today, after 81 years of colonial rule. The island adopted a parliamentary system and Earl Barrow, who led the island's Democratic Labour Party, would be the country's first Prime Minister. Barbados, 90 per cent of whose population was of African descent, counted its main exports as molasses, sugar and rum. It would maintain a remarkably stable economic and political life after gaining control over its own destiny.

Hoover: 'Oswald Acted Alone'

FBI chief J Edgar Hoover today announced that a thorough investigation of the evidence suggested that Lee Harvey Oswald, the man who shot President John Kennedy in 1963, acted alone in the killing. Oswald, who spent more than two years living in the Soviet Union, had become involved in pro-Castro activities upon his return to the US.

Oswald had protested his innocence over Kennedy's death, but was himself killed two days later by Dallas nightclub-owner Jack Ruby. The silencing of the President's presumed killer before he could testify caused rumours of a conspiracy by Cuban or Mafia influences. US officials hoped today's announcement would lay these to rest. Their wish was in vain. The JFK conspiracy industry continues unabated to this day.

Smith Rejects British Proposals

AFTER PROLONGED deliberation in the Rhodesian cabinet, rebel Prime Minister Ian Smith today delivered his government's response to British terms for settlement of the 13-month UDI (unilateral declaration of independence) dispute – a resounding 'no'.

UK Prime Minister Harold Wilson had recently met Mr Smith aboard a ship in the Mediterranean, advising him that Britain demanded he abandon UDI, give up control of Rhodesia's armed forces and allow black African representation in the cabinet.

Rhodesia's failure to accept these terms meant that the UN Security Council would almost certainly agree to impose sanctions on the rebel regime, although it was thought there was no shortage of countries willing to breach these in the name of profit, or greed.

Later in the month, the British PM announced that majority rule was the primary condition for settlement in Rhodesia: two days later Rhodesia announced that it had left the British Commonwealth. With the exception of a sympathetic South Africa, it really was alone.

1: Green Green Grass Of Home
- Tom Jones

2: What Would I Be
- Val Doonican

3: Good Vibrations
- The Beach Boys

4: Morningtown Ride
- The Seekers

5: Friday On My Mind
- The Easybeats

6: My Mind's Eye
- The Small Faces

7: Dead End Street
- The Kinks

8: Gimme Some Loving
- The Spencer Davis Group

9: What Becomes Of The Brokenhearted
- Jimmy Ruffin

10: Semi-Detached Suburban Mr Jones
- Manfred Mann

DECEMBER 3

'Take These Chains...'

Blind US blues singer Ray Charles, whose hits included *What'd I Say*, *Hit The Road Jack* and *Take These Chains From My Heart*, was today convicted on heroin and marijuana possession charges. Having stayed off drugs since his arrest earlier this year - a fact corroborated through tests - Charles's five-year jail sentence was suspended in favour of a $10,000 fine. He was also put on probation for four years.

Charles, who flew his own private jet, despite his handicap, would keep his nose clean, keep on producing memorable music and, in 1986, was one of a select few Americans to be honoured with a special Kennedy Center Award medallion, presented by President Ronald Reagan in a nationally televised ceremony.

DECEMBER 23

Ready, Steady... No Go!

The last ever edition of *Ready, Steady, Go!* was broadcast tonight, The Who bringing down the curtain – literally – on what for the past three years had been British TV's premier pop show. Manfred Mann had penned the *5-4-3-2-1* theme tune, while Cathy McGowan (pictured), who presented the Friday night show with disc jockey Keith Fordyce, established herself as one of the best-known faces of the era.

Drummer and bandleader Dave Clark, of The Dave Clark Five fame, would later buy up the rights to the show, which would be re-broadcast on the UK's Channel 4 from 1985.

DECEMBER 12

Yacht A Lot He Got!

Lone British yachtsman Francis Chichester arrived in Sydney, Australia, today - the halfway point on his single-handed global circumnavigation in the yacht *Gypsy Moth IV*.

The 65 year old would complete his self-appointed task in May 1967 and, on returning to his home soil, receive a knighthood from Her Majesty Queen Elizabeth II. The vessel which had withstood the buffetings of the world's oceans would be exhibited at Greenwich as a monument to Chichester's remarkable achievement.

DECEMBER 15

Master Cartoonist Walt Disney Dies

WALT DISNEY, legendary cartoonist and one of the earliest pioneers of children's and family entertainment, died suddenly today at the age of 65. Right from the point when Mickey Mouse, the character he created in 1928, saved his studio from the brink of financial disaster, Disney had enjoyed success after success with famous full-length animated films such as *Snow White And The Seven Dwarfs* (the first ever, in 1937, and one on which the Kansas-born draughtsman's entire savings were invested), *Pinocchio* and *One Hundred And One Dalmatians,* among many others.

Along the way, the Disney genius, and that of his superb team, also created a host of cartoon characters destined for immortality and the unfettered pleasure of generations of kids of all ages - Donald Duck, Pluto and Goofy included.

His legendary *Fantasia,* a brilliant visualization of famous classical music works, saw the first use of a stereophonic sound system, pioneered by the Disney Studios, which later became the first exclusively to use Technicolor.

In the last few years of his life, Disney made another bold move when he combined live actors (Julie Andrews and Dick Van Dyke) with animation to produce the phenomenally successful *Mary Poppins.* In the mid 1950s Disney realized another long-held dream when he opened the company's first theme park, Disneyland, in California. A similar project, to be called Disneyworld, was under way in Florida when he died.

Civilians Pay The Price In Vietnam

Following the bombing of a 'friendly' village in September and the crash by a US cargo plane onto another Vietnamese community, the Pentagon admitted that recent bombing in North Vietnam had caused widespread civilian casualties. While stressing that 'all possible care' was taken to avoid such occurrences, officials stated that the Vietcong often sited military emplacements in civilian areas.

However, 1966 also saw several fatal 'own goals' by US forces in south-east Asia. In June, a pilot admitted shooting down two South Vietnamese planes, while 20 US soldiers were killed when they were bombed with napalm by their own comrades in August.

Official figures released at the end of this month revealed that the United States' death-toll in the Vietnam conflict had now reached 6,450, while the number of troops committed to the war exceeded 340,000.

The Green, Green Grass Of Jones

Welsh pop balladeer Tom Jones ended an already successful 1966 when he began a seven-week residency atop the British charts today with his single, *Green Green Grass Of Home*.

The song, written by US country composer Claude 'Curly' Putnam Jr, was inspired by the 1950 movie *The Asphalt Jungle*, in which Marilyn Monroe made her screen début. Sterling Hayden played the gangster who, after dreaming of returning to his farm, finally made it – having meanwhile died of gunshot wounds – and was buried in the green grass he longed for.

Putnam also co-wrote the Tammy Wynette weepie *'DIVORCE'*, while Jones would register nine more Top 10 hits in Britain during the next three and a half years. The song would remain a kitsch classic.

Pink Floyd Take A Trip

A new London club, The Night Tripper, opened its doors for the first time this evening with a performance by an up-and-coming Cambridge four-piece named Pink Floyd, led by singer Syd Barrett.

Changing its name to UFO in 1967, the venue - previously an Irish dancehall called The Blarney Club - would become the capital's premier psychedelic music showcase, giving Marc Bolan and others their first exposure to press and public, which often included a Beatle or two. As for Pink Floyd, they would record their first single *Arnold Layne* in February 1967.

YOUR 1966 HOROSCOPE

Unlike most Western horoscope systems which group astrological signs into month-long periods based on the influence of 12 constellations, the Chinese believe that those born in the same year of their calendar share common qualities, traits and weaknesses with one of 12 animals - Rat, Ox, Tiger, Rabbit, Dragon, Snake, Horse, Sheep, Monkey, Rooster, Dog or Pig.

They also allocate the general attributes of five natural elements - Earth, Fire, Metal, Water, Wood - and an overall positive or negative aspect to each sign to summarize its qualities.

If you were born between February 2, 1965 and January 20, 1966, you are a Snake. As this book is devoted to the events of 1966, let's take a look at the sign which governs those born between January 21 that year and February 8, 1967 - The Year of The Horse:

THE HORSE
JANUARY 21, 1966
- FEBRUARY 8, 1967
ELEMENT: WOOD   ASPECT: (+)

Horses are born with vast inbuilt energy resources, are very strong and active, and prefer to be busy all the time. They are at their best when their stamina and physical resources are put to the test, are both quick to catch on and efficient in their undertakings.

Horses are pleasant, lively people with the ability to put people at ease instantly. Gifted with good humour and *bonhomie*, they bring good cheer to those around them.

Horses are characterized by a strong need for freedom and independence, and don't like to be tied down by commitments. As soon as someone makes too many demands or restricts their freedom, Horses will kick out, rebel and run away towards new horizons.

As they tend to act on impulse to remain their own master or mistress, there is a strong sense of unpredictability about Horses. It makes them appear very casual in their attitude to life. However, as much as they don't want their lives to be ruled by anyone but themselves, Horses are very tolerant and unresentful towards those who don't fulfil their commitments.

Despite their carefree outlook on life, Horses can be very loyal to family and friends and are not afraid of taking on necessary responsibilities. They have incisive and quick-witted minds and make accurate judgements. Being very practical and logical, they are able to deal with several projects at the same time.

Horses have a strong sense of what they should look like and are attracted to refinement and elegance in their choice of appearance. Very diplomatic, they possess extraordinary charm and fall in love easily. They find it hard to keep their own counsel - whatever they feel or think must be expressed on the spot. They find it impossible to keep secrets as gossiping and chatting are two of their favourite hobbies.

Horses are easy-going, tolerant, affable people who have the need to feel free, be able to move forward, and to accept and deal with their responsibilities.

FAMOUS HORSES

HRH Princess Margaret	rock star, philanthropist
HRH Prince Michael of Kent	(Live Aid)
Neil Armstrong	**Neil Kinnock**
astronaut	Socialist politician
Clint Eastwood	**Paul McCartney**
Oscar-winning actor, producer, director	rock singer, writer, producer
Billy Graham	**Barbra Streisand**
Christian evangelist	singer, actress, producer, director
Bob Geldof	**Chris Evert**
	tennis champion